Erechtheus by Algernon Charles Swinburne

A TRAGEDY

Algernon Charles Swinburne was born on April 5th, 1837, in London, into a wealthy Northumbrian family. He was educated at Eton and at Balliol College, Oxford, but did not complete a degree.

In 1860 Swinburne published two verse dramas but achieved his first literary success in 1865 with Atalanta in Calydon, written in the form of classical Greek tragedy. The following year "Poems and Ballads" brought him instant notoriety. He was now identified with "indecent" themes and the precept of art for art's sake.

Although he produced much after this success in general his popularity and critical reputation declined. The most important qualities of Swinburne's work are an intense lyricism, his intricately extended and evocative imagery, metrical virtuosity, rich use of assonance and alliteration, and bold, complex rhythms.

Swinburne's physical appearance was small, frail, and plagued by several other oddities of physique and temperament. Throughout the 1860s and 1870s he drank excessively and was prone to accidents that often left him bruised, bloody, or unconscious. Until his forties he suffered intermittent physical collapses that necessitated removal to his parents' home while he recovered.

Throughout his career Swinburne also published literary criticism of great worth. His deep knowledge of world literatures contributed to a critical style rich in quotation, allusion, and comparison. He is particularly noted for discerning studies of Elizabethan dramatists and of many English and French poets and novelists. As well he was a noted essayist and wrote two novels.

In 1879, Swinburne's friend and literary agent, Theodore Watts-Dunton, intervened during a time when Swinburne was dangerously ill. Watts-Dunton isolated Swinburne at a suburban home in Putney and gradually weaned him from alcohol, former companions and many other habits as well.

Much of his poetry in this period may be inferior but some individual poems are exceptional; "By the North Sea," "Evening on the Broads," "A Nympholept," "The Lake of Gaube," and "Neap-Tide."

Swinburne lived another thirty years with Watts-Dunton. He denied Swinburne's friends access to him, controlled the poet's money, and restricted his activities. It is often quoted that 'he saved the man but killed the poet'.

Swinburne died on April 10th, 1909 at the age of seventy-two.

Index of Contents

ERECHTHEUS
CHORUS OF ATHENIAN ELDERS.
PRAXITHEA
CHTHONIA
HERALD OF EUMOLPUS
MESSENGER.
ATHENIAN HERALD.
ATHENA.

ERECHTHEUS

ERECHTHEUS
Mother of life and death and all men's days,
Earth, whom I chief of all men born would bless,
And call thee with more loving lips than theirs
Mother, for of this very body of thine
And living blood I have my breath and live,
Behold me, even thy son, me crowned of men,
Me made thy child by that strong cunning God
Who fashions fire and iron, who begat
Me for a sword and beacon-fire on thee,
Me fosterling of Pallas, in her shade
Reared, that I first might pay the nursing debt,
Hallowing her fame with flower of third-year feasts,
And first bow down the bridled strength of steeds
To lose the wild wont of their birth, and bear
Clasp of man's knees and steerage of his hand,
Or fourfold service of his fire-swift wheels
That whirl the four-yoked chariot; me the king
Who stand before thee naked now, and cry,
O holy and general mother of all men born,
But mother most and motherliest of mine,
Earth, for I ask thee rather of all the Gods,
What have we done? what word mistimed or work
Hath winged the wild feet of this timeless curse
To fall as fire upon us? Lo, I stand
Here on this brow's crown of the city's head
That crowns its lovely body, till death's hour
Waste it; but now the dew of dawn and birth
Is fresh upon it from thy womb, and we
Behold it born how beauteous; one day more
I see the world's wheel of the circling sun

Roll up rejoicing to regard on earth
This one thing goodliest, fair as heaven or he,
Worth a God's gaze or strife of Gods; but now
Would this day's ebb of their spent wave of strife
Sweep it to sea, wash it on wreck, and leave
A costless thing contemned; and in our stead,
Where these walls were and sounding streets of men,
Make wide a waste for tongueless water-herds
And spoil of ravening fishes; that no more
Should men say, Here was Athens. This shalt thou
Sustain not, nor thy son endure to see,
Nor thou to live and look on; for the womb
Bare me not base that bare me miserable,
To hear this loud brood of the Thracian foam
Break its broad strength of billowy-beating war
Here, and upon it as a blast of death
Blowing, the keen wrath of a fire-souled king,
A strange growth grafted on our natural soil,
A root of Thrace in Eleusinian earth
Set for no comfort to the kindly land,
Son of the sea's lord and our first-born foe,
Eumolpus; nothing sweet in ears of thine
The music of his making, nor a song
Toward hopes of ours auspicious; for the note
Rings as for death oracular to thy sons
That goes before him on the sea-wind blown
Full of this charge laid on me, to put out
The brief light kindled of mine own child's life,
Or with this helmsman hand that steers the state
Run right on the under shoal and ridge of death
The populous ship with all its fraughtage gone
And sails that were to take the wind of time
Rent, and the tackling that should hold out fast
In confluent surge of loud calamities
Broken, with spars of rudders and lost oars
That were to row toward harbour and find rest
In some most glorious haven of all the world
And else may never near it: such a song
The Gods have set his lips on fire withal
Who threatens now in all their names to bring
Ruin; but none of these, thou knowest, have I
Chid with my tongue or cursed at heart for grief,
Knowing how the soul runs reinless on sheer death
Whose grief or joy takes part against the Gods.
And what they will is more than our desire,
And their desire is more than what we will.
For no man's will and no desire of man's
Shall stand as doth a God's will. Yet, O fair

Mother, that seest me how I cast no word
Against them, plead no reason, crave no cause,
Boast me not blameless, nor beweep me wronged,
By this fair wreath of towers we have decked thee with,
This chaplet that we give thee woven of walls,
This girdle of gate and temple and citadel
Drawn round beneath thy bosom, and fast linked
As to thine heart's root—this dear crown of thine,
This present light, this city—be not thou
Slow to take heed nor slack to strengthen her,
Fare we so short-lived howsoe'er, and pay
What price we may to ransom thee thy town,
Not me my life; but thou that diest not, thou,
Though all our house die for this people's sake,
Keep thou for ours thy crown our city, guard
And give it life the lovelier that we died.

CHORUS
Sun, that hast lightened and loosed by thy might
Ocean and Earth from the lordship of night,
Quickening with vision his eye that was veiled,
Freshening the force in her heart that had failed,
That sister fettered and blinded brother
Should have sight by thy grace and delight of each other,
Behold now and see
What profit is given them of thee;
What wrath has enkindled with madness of mind
Her limbs that were bounden, his face that was blind,
To be locked as in wrestle together, and lighten
With fire that shall darken thy fire in the sky,
Body to body and eye against eye
In a war against kind,
Till the bloom of her fields and her high hills whiten
With the foam of his waves more high.
For the sea-marks set to divide of old
The kingdoms to Ocean and Earth assigned,
The hoar sea-fields from the cornfields' gold,
His wine-bright waves from her vineyards' fold,
Frail forces we find
To bridle the spirit of Gods or bind
Till the heat of their hearts wax cold.
But the peace that was stablished between them to stand
Is rent now in twain by the strength of his hand
Who stirs up the storm of his sons overbold
To pluck from fight what he lost of right,
By council and judgment of Gods that spake
And gave great Pallas the strife's fair stake,

The lordship and love of the lovely land,
The grace of the town that hath on it for crown
But a headband to wear
Of violets one-hued with her hair:
For the vales and the green high places of earth
Hold nothing so fair,
And the depths of the sea bear no such birth
Of the manifold births they bear.
Too well, too well was the great stake worth
A strife divine for the Gods to judge,
A crowned God's triumph, a foiled God's grudge,
Though the loser be strong and the victress wise
Who played long since for so large a prize,
The fruitful immortal anointed adored
Dear city of men without master or lord,
Fair fortress and fostress of sons born free,
Who stand in her sight and in thine, O sun,
Slaves of no man, subjects of none;
A wonder enthroned on the hills and sea,
A maiden crowned with a fourfold glory
That none from the pride of her head may rend,
Violet and olive-leaf purple and hoary,
Song-wreath and story the fairest of fame,
Flowers that the winter can blast not or bend;
A light upon earth as the sun's own flame,
A name as his name,
Athens, a praise without end.

A noise is arisen against us of waters,   [Strophe 1.
A sound as of battle come up from the sea.
Strange hunters are hard on us, hearts without pity;
They have staked their nets round the fair young city,
That the sons of her strength and her virgin daughters
Should find not whither alive to flee.
And we know not yet of the word unwritten,   [Antistrophe 1.
The doom of the Pythian we have not heard;
From the navel of earth and the veiled mid altar
We wait for a token with hopes that falter,
With fears that hang on our hearts thought-smitten
Lest her tongue be kindled with no good word.
O thou not born of the womb, nor bred   [Strophe 2.
In the bride-night's warmth of a changed God's bed,
But thy life as a lightning was flashed from the light of thy
father's head,
O chief God's child by a motherless birth,
If aught in thy sight we indeed be worth,
Keep death from us thou, that art none of the Gods of the dead
under earth.

Thou that hast power on us, save, if thou wilt;
Let the blind wave breach not thy wall scarce built;
But bless us not so as by bloodshed, impute not for grace to us guilt,
Nor by price of pollution of blood set us free;
Let the hands be taintless that clasp thy knee,
Nor a maiden be slain to redeem for a maiden her shrine from the sea.
O earth, O sun, turn back
Full on his deadly track
Death, that would smite you black and mar your creatures,
And with one hand disroot
All tender flower and fruit,
With one strike blind and mute the heaven's fair features,
Pluck out the eyes of morn, and make
Silence in the east and blackness whence the bright songs break.
Help, earth, help, heaven, that hear
The song-notes of our fear,
Shrewd notes and shrill, not clear or joyful-sounding;
Hear, highest of Gods, and stay
Death on his hunter's way,
Full on his forceless prey his beagles hounding;
Break thou his bow, make short his hand,
Maim his fleet foot whose passage kills the living land.
Let a third wave smite not us, father,
Long since sore smitten of twain,
Lest the house of thy son's son perish
And his name be barren on earth.
Whose race wilt thou comfort rather
If none to thy son remain?
Whose seed wilt thou choose to cherish
If his be cut off in the birth?
For the first fair graft of his graffing
Was rent from its maiden root
By the strong swift hand of a lover
Who fills the night with his breath;
On the lip of the stream low-laughing
Her green soft virginal shoot
Was plucked from the stream-side cover
By the grasp of a love like death.
For a God's was the mouth that kissed her
Who speaks, and the leaves lie dead,
When winter awakes as at warning
To the sound of his foot from Thrace.
Nor happier the bed of her sister
Though Love's self laid her abed
By a bridegroom beloved of the morning
And fair as the dawn's own face.
For Procris, ensnared and ensnaring
By the fraud of a twofold wile,

With the point of her own spear stricken
By the gift of her own hand fell.
Oversubtle in doubts, overdaring
In deeds and devices of guile,
And strong to quench as to quicken,
O Love, have we named thee well?
By thee was the spear's edge whetted   [Strophe 6.
That laid her dead in the dew,
In the moist green glens of the midland
By her dear lord slain and thee.
And him at the cliff's end fretted
By the grey keen waves, him too,
Thine hand from the white-browed headland
Flung down for a spoil to the sea.
But enough now of griefs grey-growing   [Antistrophe 6.
Have darkened the house divine,
Have flowered on its boughs and faded,
And green is the brave stock yet.
O father all-seeing and all-knowing,
Let the last fruit fall not of thine
From the tree with whose boughs we are shaded,
From the stock that thy son's hand set.

ERECHTHEUS
O daughter of Cephisus, from all time
Wise have I found thee, wife and queen, of heart
Perfect; nor in the days that knew not wind
Nor days when storm blew death upon our peace
Was thine heart swoln with seed of pride, or bowed
With blasts of bitter fear that break men's souls
Who lift too high their minds toward heaven, in thought
Too godlike grown for worship; but of mood
Equal, in good time reverent of time bad,
And glad in ill days of the good that were.
Nor now too would I fear thee, now misdoubt
Lest fate should find thee lesser than thy doom,
Chosen if thou be to bear and to be great
Haply beyond all women; and the word
Speaks thee divine, dear queen, that speaks thee dead,
Dead being alive, or quick and dead in one
Shall not men call thee living? yet I fear
To slay thee timeless with my proper tongue,
With lips, thou knowest, that love thee; and such work
Was never laid of Gods on men, such word
No mouth of man learnt ever, as from mine
Most loth to speak thine ear most loth shall take
And hold it hateful as the grave to hear.

PRAXITHEA

That word there is not in all speech of man,
King, that being spoken of the Gods and thee
I have not heart to honour, or dare hold
More than I hold thee or the Gods in hate
Hearing; but if my heart abhor it heard
Being insubmissive, hold me not thy wife
But use me like a stranger, whom thine hand
Hath fed by chance and finding thence no thanks
Flung off for shame's sake to forgetfulness.

ERECHTHEUS

O, of what breath shall such a word be made,
Or from what heart find utterance? Would my tongue
Were rent forth rather from the quivering root
Than made as fire or poison thus for thee.

PRAXITHEA

But if thou speak of blood, and I that hear
Be chosen of all for this land's love to die
And save to thee thy city, know this well,
Happiest I hold me of her seed alive.

ERECHTHEUS

O sun that seest, what saying was this of thine,
God, that thy power has breathed into my lips?
For from no sunlit shrine darkling it came.

PRAXITHEA

What portent from the mid oracular place
Hath smitten thee so like a curse that flies
Wingless, to waste men with its plagues? yet speak.

ERECHTHEUS

Thy blood the Gods require not; take this first.

PRAXITHEA

To me than thee more grievous this should sound.

ERECHTHEUS

That word rang truer and bitterer than it knew.

PRAXITHEA

This is not then thy grief, to see me die?

ERECHTHEUS

Die shalt thou not, yet give thy blood to death.

PRAXITHEA

If this ring worse I know not; strange it rang.

ERECHTHEUS

Alas, thou knowest not; woe is me that know.

PRAXITHEA

And woe shall mine be, knowing; yet halt not here.

ERECHTHEUS

Guiltless of blood this state may stand no more.

PRAXITHEA

Firm let it stand whatever bleed or fall.

ERECHTHEUS

O Gods, that I should say it shall and weep.

PRAXITHEA

Weep, and say this? no tears should bathe such words.

ERECHTHEUS

Woe's me that I must weep upon them, woe.

PRAXITHEA

What stain is on them for thy tears to cleanse?

ERECHTHEUS

A stain of blood unpurgeable with tears.

PRAXITHEA

Whence? for thou sayest it is and is not mine.

ERECHTHEUS

Hear then and know why only of all men I
That bring such news as mine is, I alone
Must wash good words with weeping; I and thou,
Woman, must wail to hear men sing, must groan
To see their joy who love us; all our friends
Save only we, and all save we that love
This holiness of Athens, in our sight
Shall lift their hearts up, in our hearing praise
Gods whom we may not; for to these they give
Life of their children, flower of all their seed,
For all their travail fruit, for all their hopes
Harvest; but we for all our good things, we
Have at their hands which fill all these folk full
Death, barrenness, child-slaughter, curses, cares,

Sea-leaguer and land-shipwreck; which of these,
Which wilt thou first give thanks for? all are thine.

PRAXITHEA

What first they give who give this city good,
For that first given to save it I give thanks
First, and thanks heartier from a happier tongue,
More than for any my peculiar grace
Shown me and not my country; next for this,
That none of all these but for all these I
Must bear my burden, and no eye but mine
Weep of all women's in this broad land born
Who see their land's deliverance; but much more,
But most for this I thank them most of all,
That this their edge of doom is chosen to pierce
My heart and not my country's; for the sword
Drawn to smite there and sharpened for such stroke
Should wound more deep than any turned on me.

CHORUS

Well fares the land that bears such fruit, and well
The spirit that breeds such thought and speech in man.

ERECHTHEUS

O woman, thou hast shamed my heart with thine,
To show so strong a patience; take then all;
For all shall break not nor bring down thy soul.
The word that journeying to the bright God's shrine
Who speaks askance and darkling, but his name
Hath in it slaying and ruin broad writ out,
I heard, hear thou: thus saith he; There shall die
One soul for all this people; from thy womb
Came forth the seed that here on dry bare ground
Death's hand must sow untimely, to bring forth
Nor blade nor shoot in season, being by name
To the under Gods made holy, who require
For this land's life her death and maiden blood
To save a maiden city. Thus I heard,
And thus with all said leave thee; for save this
No word is left us, and no hope alive.

CHORUS

He hath uttered too surely his wrath not obscurely, nor wrapt as in mists of his breath,   [**Strophe**.
The master that lightens not hearts he enlightens, but gives them foreknowledge of death.
As a bolt from the cloud hath he sent it aloud and proclaimed it afar,
From the darkness and height of the horror of night hath he shown us a star.
Star may I name it and err not, or flame shall I say,
Born of the womb that was born for the tomb of the day?

O Night, whom other but thee for mother, and Death for the father,
Night,   [Antistrophe.
Shall we dream to discover, save thee and thy lover, to bring such a sorrow to sight?
From the slumberless bed for thy bedfellow spread and his bride under earth
Hast thou brought forth a wild and insatiable child, an unbearable birth.
Fierce are the fangs of his wrath, and the pangs that they give;
None is there, none that may bear them, not one that would live.

CHTHONIA

Forth of the fine-spun folds of veils that hide
My virgin chamber toward the full-faced sun
I set my foot not moved of mine own will,
Unmaidenlike, nor with unprompted speed
Turn eyes too broad or doglike unabashed
On reverend heads of men and thence on thine,
Mother, now covered from the light and bowed
As hers who mourns her brethren; but what grief
Bends thy blind head thus earthward, holds thus mute,
I know not till thy will be to lift up
Toward mine thy sorrow-muffled eyes and speak;
And till thy will be would I know this not.

PRAXITHEA

Old men and childless, or if sons ye have seen
And daughters, elder-born were these than mine,
Look on this child, how young of years, how sweet,
How scant of time and green of age her life
Puts forth its flower of girlhood; and her gait
How virginal, how soft her speech, her eyes
How seemly smiling; wise should all ye be,
All honourable and kindly men of age;
Now give me counsel and one word to say
That I may bear to speak, and hold my peace
Henceforth for all time even as all ye now.
Dumb are ye all, bowed eyes and tongueless mouths,
Unprofitable; if this were wind that speaks,
As much its breath might move you. Thou then, child,
Set thy sweet eyes on mine; look through them well;
Take note of all the writing of my face
As of a tablet or a tomb inscribed
That bears me record; lifeless now, my life
Thereon that was think written; brief to read,
Yet shall the scripture sear thine eyes as fire
And leave them dark as dead men's. Nay, dear child,
Thou hast no skill, my maiden, and no sense
To take such knowledge; sweet is all thy lore,
And all this bitter; yet I charge thee learn
And love and lay this up within thine heart,

Even this my word; less ill it were to die
Than live and look upon thy mother dead,
Thy mother-land that bare thee; no man slain
But him who hath seen it shall men count unblest,
None blest as him who hath died and seen it not.

CHTHONIA
That sight some God keep from me though I die.

PRAXITHEA
A God from thee shall keep it; fear not this.

CHTHONIA
Thanks all my life long shall he gain of mine.

PRAXITHEA
Short gain of all yet shall he get of thee.

CHTHONIA
Brief be my life, yet so long live my thanks.

PRAXITHEA
So long? so little; how long shall they live?

CHTHONIA
Even while I see the sunlight and thine eyes.

PRAXITHEA
Would mine might shut ere thine upon the sun.

CHTHONIA
For me thou prayest unkindly; change that prayer.

PRAXITHEA
Not well for me thou sayest, and ill for thee.

CHTHONIA
Nay, for me well, if thou shalt live, not I.

PRAXITHEA
How live, and lose these loving looks of thine?

CHTHONIA
It seems I too, thus praying, then, love thee not.

PRAXITHEA
Lov'st thou not life? what wouldst thou do to die?

CHTHONIA
Well, but not more than all things, love I life.

PRAXITHEA
And fain wouldst keep it as thine age allows?

CHTHONIA
Fain would I live, and fain not fear to die.

PRAXITHEA
That I might bid thee die not! Peace; no more.

CHORUS
A godlike race of grief the Gods have set
For these to run matched equal, heart with heart.

PRAXITHEA
Child of the chief of Gods, and maiden crowned,
Queen of these towers and fostress of their king,
Pallas, and thou my father's holiest head,
A living well of life nor stanched nor stained,
O God Cephisus, thee too charge I next,
Be to me judge and witness; nor thine ear
Shall now my tongue invoke not, thou to me
Most hateful of things holy, mournfullest
Of all old sacred streams that wash the world,
Ilissus, on whose marge at flowery play
A whirlwind-footed bridegroom found my child
And rapt her northward where mine elder-born
Keeps now the Thracian bride-bed of a God
Intolerable to seamen, but this land
Finds him in hope for her sake favourable,
A gracious son by wedlock; hear me then
Thou likewise, if with no faint heart or false
The word I say be said, the gift be given,
Which might I choose I had rather die than give
Or speak and die not. Ere thy limbs were made
Or thine eyes lightened, strife, thou knowest, my child,
'Twixt God and God had risen, which heavenlier name
Should here stand hallowed, whose more liberal grace
Should win this city's worship, and our land
To which of these do reverence; first the lord
Whose wheels make lightnings of the foam-flowered sea
Here on this rock, whose height brow-bound with dawn
Is head and heart of Athens, one sheer blow
Struck, and beneath the triple wound that shook
The stony sinews and stark roots of the earth
Sprang toward the sun a sharp salt fount, and sank

Where lying it lights the heart up of the hill,
A well of bright strange brine; but she that reared
Thy father with her same chaste fostering hand
Set for a sign against it in our guard
The holy bloom of the olive, whose hoar leaf
High in the shadowy shrine of Pandrosus
Hath honour of us all; and of this strife
The twelve most high Gods judging with one mouth
Acclaimed her victress; wroth whereat, as wronged
That she should hold from him such prize and place,
The strong king of the tempest-rifted sea
Loosed reinless on the low Thriasian plain
The thunders of his chariots, swallowing stunned
Earth, beasts, and men, the whole blind foundering world
That was the sun's at morning, and ere noon
Death's; nor this only prey fulfilled his mind;
For with strange crook-toothed prows of Carian folk
Who snatch a sanguine life out of the sea,
Thieves keen to pluck their bloody fruit of spoil
From the grey fruitless waters, has their God
Furrowed our shores to waste them, as the fields
Were landward harried from the north with swords
Aonian, sickles of man-slaughtering edge
Ground for no hopeful harvest of live grain
Against us in Bœotia; these being spent,
Now this third time his wind of wrath has blown
Right on this people a mightier wave of war,
Three times more huge a ruin; such its ridge
Foam-rimmed and hollow like the womb of heaven,
But black for shining, and with death for life
Big now to birth and ripe with child, full-blown
With fear and fruit of havoc, takes the sun
Out of our eyes, darkening the day, and blinds
The fair sky's face unseasonably with change,
A cloud in one and billow of battle, a surge
High reared as heaven with monstrous surf of spears
That shake on us their shadow, till men's heads
Bend, and their hearts even with its forward wind
Wither, so blasts all seed in them of hope
Its breath and blight of presage; yea, even now
The winter of this wind out of the deeps
Makes cold our trust in comfort of the Gods
And blind our eye toward outlook; yet not here,
Here never shall the Thracian plant on high
For ours his father's symbol, nor with wreaths
A strange folk wreathe it upright set and crowned
Here where our natural people born behold
The golden Gorgon of the shield's defence

That screens their flowering olive, nor strange Gods
Be graced, and Pallas here have praise no more.
And if this be not I must give my child,
Thee, mine own very blood and spirit of mine,
Thee to be slain. Turn from me, turn thine eyes
A little from me; I can bear not yet
To see if still they smile on mine or no,
If fear make faint the light in them, or faith
Fix them as stars of safety. Need have we,
Sore need of stars that set not in mid storm,
Lights that outlast the lightnings; yet my heart
Endures not to make proof of thine or these,
Not yet to know thee whom I made, and bare
What manner of woman; had I borne thee man,
I had made no question of thine eyes or heart,
Nor spared to read the scriptures in them writ,
Wert thou my son; yet couldst thou then but die
Fallen in sheer fight by chance and charge of spears
And have no more of memory, fill no tomb
More famous than thy fellows in fair field,
Where many share the grave, many the praise;
But one crown shall one only girl my child
Wear, dead for this dear city, and give back life
To him that gave her and to me that bare,
And save two sisters living; and all this,
Is this not all good? I shall give thee, child,
Thee but by fleshly nature mine, to bleed
For dear land's love; but if the city fall
What part is left me in my children then?
But if it stand and thou for it lie dead,
Then hast thou in it a better part than we,
A holier portion than we all; for each
Hath but the length of his own life to live,
And this most glorious mother-land on earth
To worship till that life have end; but thine
Hath end no more than hers; thou, dead, shalt live
Till Athens live not; for the days and nights
Given of thy bare brief dark dividual life,
Shall she give thee half all her agelong own
And all its glory; for thou givest her these;
But with one hand she takes and gives again
More than I gave or she requires of thee.
Come therefore, I will make thee fit for death,
I that could give thee, dear, no gift at birth
Save of light life that breathes and bleeds, even I
Will help thee to this better gift than mine
And lead thee by this little living hand
That death shall make so strong, to that great end

Whence it shall lighten like a God's, and strike
Dead the strong heart of battle that would break
Athens; but ye, pray for this land, old men,
That it may bring forth never child on earth
To love it less, for none may more, than we.

CHORUS

Out of the north wind grief came forth,   [Strophe 1.
And the shining of a sword out of the sea.
Yea, of old the first-blown blast blew the prelude of this last,
The blast of his trumpet upon Rhodope.
Out of the north skies full of his cloud,
With the clamour of his storms as of a crowd
At the wheels of a great king crying aloud,
At the axle of a strong king's car
That has girded on the girdle of war—
With hands that lightened the skies in sunder
And feet whose fall was followed of thunder,
A God, a great God strange of name,
With horse-yoke fleeter-hoofed than flame,
To the mountain bed of a maiden came,
Oreithyia, the bride mismated,
Wofully wed in a snow-strewn bed
With a bridegroom that kisses the bride's mouth dead;
Without garland, without glory, without song,
As a fawn by night on the hills belated,
Given over for a spoil unto the strong.
From lips how pale so keen a wail   [Antistrophe 1.
At the grasp of a God's hand on her she gave,
When his breath that darkens air made a havoc of her hair,
It rang from the mountain even to the wave;
Rang with a cry, Woe's me, woe is me!
From the darkness upon Hæmus to the sea:
And with hands that clung to her new lord's knee,
As a virgin overborne with shame,
She besought him by her spouseless fame,
By the blameless breasts of a maid unmarried
And locks unmaidenly rent and harried,
And all her flower of body, born
To match the maidenhood of morn,
With the might of the wind's wrath wrenched and torn.
Vain, all vain as a dead man's vision
Falling by night in his old friends' sight,
To be scattered with slumber and slain ere light;
Such a breath of such a bridegroom in that hour
Of her prayers made mock, of her fears derision,
And a ravage of her youth as of a flower.
With a leap of his limbs as a lion's, a cry from his lips as of thunder,   [Strophe 2.

In a storm of amorous godhead filled with fire,
From the height of the heaven that was rent with the roar of his coming in sunder,
Sprang the strong God on the spoil of his desire.
And the pines of the hills were as green reeds shattered,
And their branches as buds of the soft spring scattered,
And the west wind and east, and the sound of the south,
Fell dumb at the blast of the north wind's mouth,
At the cry of his coming out of heaven.
And the wild beasts quailed in the rifts and hollows
Where hound nor clarion of huntsman follows,
And the depths of the sea were aghast, and whitened,
And the crowns of their waves were as flame that lightened,
And the heart of the floods thereof was riven.
But she knew not him coming for terror, she felt not her wrong that he wrought her,   **[Antistrophe 2.**
When her locks as leaves were shed before his breath,
And she heard not for terror his prayer, though the cry was a
God's that besought her,
Blown from lips that strew the world-wide seas with death.
For the heart was molten within her to hear,
And her knees beneath her were loosened for fear,
And her blood fast bound as a frost-bound water,
And the soft new bloom of the green earth's daughter
Wind-wasted as blossom of a tree;
As the wild God rapt her from earth's breast lifted,
On the strength of the stream of his dark breath drifted,
From the bosom of earth as a bride from the mother,
With storm for bridesman and wreck for brother,
As a cloud that he sheds upon the sea.

Of this hoary-headed woe   **[Epode.**
Song made memory long ago;
Now a younger grief to mourn
Needs a new song younger born.
Who shall teach our tongues to reach
What strange height of saddest speech,
For the new bride's sake that is given to be
A stay to fetter the foot of the sea,
Lest it quite spurn down and trample the town,
Ere the violets be dead that were plucked for its crown,
Or its olive-leaf whiten and wither?
Who shall say of the wind's way
That he journeyed yesterday,
Or the track of the storm that shall sound to-morrow,
If the new be more than the grey-grown sorrow?
For the wind of the green first season was keen,
And the blast shall be sharper than blew between
That the breath of the sea blows hither.

HERALD OF EUMOLPUS

Old men, grey borderers on the march of death,
Tongue-fighters, tough of talk and sinewy speech,
Else nerveless, from no crew of such faint folk
Whose tongues are stouter than their hands come I
To bid not you to battle; let them strike
Whose swords are sharper than your keen-tongued wail,
And ye, sit fast and sorrow; but what man
Of all this land-folk and earth-labouring herd
For heart or hand seems foremost, him I call
If heart be his to hearken, him bid forth
To try if one be in the sun's sight born
Of all that grope and grovel on dry ground
That may join hands in battle-grip for death
With them whose seed and strength is of the sea.

CHORUS

Know thou this much for all thy loud blast blown,
We lack not hands to speak with, swords to plead,
For proof of peril, not of boisterous breath,
Sea-wind and storm of barren mouths that foam
And rough rock's edge of menace; and short space
May lesson thy large ignorance and inform
This insolence with knowledge if there live
Men earth-begotten of no tenderer thews
Than knit the great joints of the grim sea's brood
With hasps of steel together; heaven to help,
One man shall break, even on their own flood's verge,
That iron bulk of battle; but thine eye
That sees it now swell higher than sand or shore
Haply shall see not when thine host shall shrink.

HERALD OF EUMOLPUS

Not haply, nay, but surely, shall not thine.

CHORUS

That lot shall no God give who fights for thee.

HERALD OF EUMOLPUS

Shall Gods bear bit and bridle, fool, of men?

CHORUS

Nor them forbid we nor shalt thou constrain.

HERALD OF EUMOLPUS

Yet say'st thou none shall make the good lot mine?

CHORUS

Of thy side none, nor moved for fear of thee.

HERALD OF EUMOLPUS
Gods hast thou then to baffle Gods of ours?

CHORUS
Nor thine nor mine, but equal-souled are they.

HERALD OF EUMOLPUS
Toward good and ill, then, equal-eyed of soul?

CHORUS
Nay, but swift-eyed to note where ill thoughts breed.

HERALD OF EUMOLPUS
Thy shaft word-feathered flies yet far of me.

CHORUS
Pride knows not, wounded, till the heart be cleft.

HERALD OF EUMOLPUS
No shaft wounds deep whose wing is plumed with words.

CHORUS
Lay that to heart, and bid thy tongue learn grace.

HERALD OF EUMOLPUS
Grace shall thine own crave soon too late of mine.

CHORUS
Boast thou till then, but I wage words no more.

ERECHTHEUS
Man, what shrill wind of speech and wrangling air
Blows in our ears a summons from thy lips
Winged with what message, or what gift or grace
Requiring? none but what his hand may take
Here may the foe think hence to reap, nor this
Except some doom from Godward yield it him.

HERALD OF EUMOLPUS
King of this land-folk, by my mouth to thee
Thus saith the son of him that shakes thine earth,
Eumolpus; now the stakes of war are set,
For land or sea to win by throw and wear;
Choose therefore or to quit thy side and give
The palm unfought for to his bloodless hand,
Or by that father's sceptre, and the foot

Whose tramp far off makes tremble for pure fear
Thy soul-struck mother, piercing like a sword
The immortal womb that bare thee; by the waves
That no man bridles and that bound thy world,
And by the winds and storms of all the sea,
He swears to raze from eyeshot of the sun
This city named not of his father's name,
And wash to deathward down one flood of doom
This whole fresh brood of earth yeaned naturally,
Green yet and faint in its first blade, unblown
With yellow hope of harvest; so do thou,
Seeing whom thy time is come to meet, for fear
Yield, or gird up thy force to fight and die.

ERECHTHEUS
To fight then be it; for if to die or live,
No man but only a God knows this much yet
Seeing us fare forth, who bear but in our hands
The weapons not the fortunes of our fight;
For these now rest as lots that yet undrawn
Lie in the lap of the unknown hour; but this
I know, not thou, whose hollow mouth of storm
Is but a warlike wind, a sharp salt breath
That bites and wounds not; death nor life of mine
Shall give to death or lordship of strange kings
The soul of this live city, nor their heel
Bruise her dear brow discrowned, nor snaffle or goad
Wound her free mouth or stain her sanguine side
Yet masterless of man; so bid thy lord
Learn ere he weep to learn it, and too late
Gnash teeth that could not fasten on her flesh,
And foam his life out in dark froth of blood
Vain as a wind's waif of the loud-mouthed sea
Torn from the wave's edge whitening. Tell him this;
Though thrice his might were mustered for our scathe
And thicker set with fence of thorn-edged spears
Than sands are whirled about the wintering beach
When storms have swoln the rivers, and their blasts
Have breached the broad sea-banks with stress of sea,
That waves of inland and the main make war
As men that mix and grapple; though his ranks
Were more to number than all wildwood leaves
The wind waves on the hills of all the world,
Yet should the heart not faint, the head not fall,
The breath not fail of Athens. Say, the Gods
From lips that have no more on earth to say
Have told thee this the last good news or ill
That I shall speak in sight of earth and sun

Or he shall hear and see them: for the next
That ear of his from tongue of mine may take
Must be the first word spoken underground
From dead to dead in darkness. Hence; make haste,
Lest war's fleet foot be swifter than thy tongue
And I that part not to return again
On him that comes not to depart away
Be fallen before thee; for the time is full,
And with such mortal hope as knows not fear
I go this high last way to the end of all.

CHORUS

Who shall put a bridle in the mourner's lips to chasten them,	[Strophe 1.

Who shall put a bridle in the mourner's lips to chasten them,   **[Strophe 1.**
Or seal up the fountains of his tears for shame?
Song nor prayer nor prophecy shall slacken tears nor hasten them,
Till grief be within him as a burnt-out flame;
Till the passion be broken in his breast
And the might thereof molten into rest,
And the rain of eyes that weep be dry,
And the breath be stilled of lips that sigh.
Death at last for all men is a harbour; yet they flee from it,   **[Antistrophe 1.**
Set sails to the storm-wind and again to sea;
Yet for all their labour no whit further shall they be from it,
Nor longer but wearier shall their life's work be.
And with anguish of travail until night
Shall they steer into shipwreck out of sight,
And with oars that break and shrouds that strain
Shall they drive whence no ship steers again.
Bitter and strange is the word of the God most high,   **[Strophe 2.**
And steep the strait of his way.
Through a pass rock-rimmed and narrow the light that gleams
On the faces of men falls faint as the dawn of dreams,
The dayspring of death as a star in an under sky
Where night is the dead men's day.
As darkness and storm is his will that on earth is done,   **[Antistrophe 2.**
As a cloud is the face of his strength.
King of kings, holiest of holies, and mightiest of might,
Lord of the lords of thine heaven that are humble in thy sight,
Hast thou set not an end for the path of the fires of the sun,
To appoint him a rest at length?
Hast thou told not by measure the waves of the waste wide sea,   **[Strophe 3.**
And the ways of the wind their master and thrall to thee?
Hast thou filled not the furrows with fruit for the world's increase?
Has thine ear not heard from of old or thine eye not read
The thought and the deed of us living, the doom of us dead?
Hast thou made not war upon earth, and again made peace?
Therefore, O father, that seest us whose lives are a breath,   **[Antistrophe 3.**
Take off us thy burden, and give us not wholly to death.

For lovely is life, and the law wherein all things live,
And gracious the season of each, and the hour of its kind,
And precious the seed of his life in a wise man's mind;
But all save life for his life will a base man give.
But a life that is given for the life of the whole live land,   [Strophe 4.
From a heart unspotted a gift of a spotless hand,
Of pure will perfect and free, for the land's life's sake,
What man shall fear not to put forth his hand and take?
For the fruit of a sweet life plucked in its pure green prime   [Antistrophe 4.
On his hand who plucks is as blood, on his soul as crime.
With cursing ye buy not blessing, nor peace with strife,
And the hand is hateful that chaffers with death for life.
Hast thou heard, O my heart, and endurest   [Strophe 5.
The word that is said,
What a garland by sentence found surest
Is wrought for what head?
With what blossomless flowerage of sea-foam and blood-coloured foliage inwound
It shall crown as a heifer's for slaughter the forehead for marriage uncrowned?
How the veils and the wreaths that should cover   [Antistrophe 5.
The brows of the bride
Shall be shed by the breath of what lover
And scattered aside?
With a blast of the mouth of what bridegroom the crowns shall be cast from her hair,
And her head by what altar made humble be left of them naked and bare?
At a shrine unbeloved of a God unbeholden a gift shall be given for the land,   [Strophe 6.
That its ramparts though shaken with clamour and horror of manifold waters may stand;
That the crests of its citadels crowned and its turrets that thrust up their heads to the sun
May behold him unblinded with darkness of waves overmastering their bulwarks begun.
As a bride shall they bring her, a prey for the bridegroom, a flower for the couch of her lord;   [Ant 6.
They shall muffle her mouth that she cry not or curse them, and cover her eyes from the sword.
They shall fasten her lips as with bit and with bridle, and darken the light of her face,
That the soul of the slayer may not falter, his heart be not molten, his hand give not grace.
If she weep then, yet may none that hear take pity;   [Strophe 7.
If she cry not, none should hearken though she cried.
Shall a virgin shield thine head for love, O city,
With a virgin's blood anointed as for pride?
Yet we held thee dear and hallowed of her favour,   [Antistrophe 7.
Dear of all men held thy people to her heart;
Nought she loves the breath of blood, the sanguine savour,
Who hath built with us her throne and chosen her part.
Bloodless are her works, and sweet   [Epode.
All the ways that feel her feet;
From the empire of her eyes
Light takes life and darkness flies;
From the harvest of her hands
Wealth strikes root in prosperous lands;
Wisdom of her word is made;
At her strength is strength afraid;

From the beam of her bright spear
War's fleet foot goes back for fear;
In her shrine she reared the birth
Fire-begotten on live earth;
Glory from her helm was shed
On his olive-shadowed head;
By no hand but his shall she
Scourge the storms back of the sea,
To no fame but his shall give
Grace, being dead, with hers to live,
And in double name divine
Half the godhead of their shrine.
But now with what word, with what woe may we meet
The timeless passage of piteous feet,
Hither that bend to the last way's end
They shall walk upon earth?
What song be rolled for a bride black-stoled
And the mother whose hand of her hand hath hold?
For anguish of heart is my soul's strength broken
And the tongue sealed fast that would fain have spoken,
To behold thee, O child of so bitter a birth
That we counted so sweet,
What way thy steps to what bride-feast tend,
What gift he must give that shall wed thee for token
If the bridegroom be goodly to greet.

CHTHONIA
People, old men of my city, lordly wise and hoar of head,
I a spouseless bride and crownless but with garlands of the dead
From the fruitful light turn silent to my dark unchilded bed.

CHORUS
Wise of word was he too surely, but with deadlier wisdom wise,
First who gave thee name from under earth, no breath from upper skies,
When, foredoomed to this day's darkness, their first daylight filled thine eyes.

PRAXITHEA
Child, my child that wast and art but death's and now no more of mine,
Half my heart is cloven with anguish by the sword made sharp for thine,
Half exalts its wing for triumph, that I bare thee thus divine.

CHTHONIA
Though for me the sword's edge thirst that sets no point against thy breast,
Mother, O my mother, where I drank of life and fell on rest,
Thine, not mine, is all the grief that marks this hour accurst and blest.

CHORUS
Sweet thy sleep and sweet the bosom was that gave thee sleep and birth;

Harder now the breast, and girded with no marriage-band for girth,
Where thine head shall sleep, the namechild of the lords of under earth.

PRAXITHEA
Dark the name and dark the gifts they gave thee, child, in childbirth were,
Sprung from him that rent the womb of earth, a bitter seed to bear,
Born with groanings of the ground that gave him way toward heaven's dear air.

CHTHONIA
Day to day makes answer, first to last, and life to death; but I,
Born for death's sake, die for life's sake, if indeed this be to die,
This my doom that seals me deathless till the springs of time run dry.

CHORUS
Children shalt thou bear to memory, that to man shalt bring forth none;
Yea, the lordliest that lift eyes and hearts and songs to meet the sun,
Names to fire men's ears like music till the round world's race be run.

PRAXITHEA
I thy mother, named of Gods that wreak revenge and brand with blame,
Now for thy love shall be loved as thou, and famous with thy fame,
While this city's name on earth shall be for earth her mightiest name.

CHTHONIA
That I may give this poor girl's blood of mine
Scarce yet sun-warmed with summer, this thin life
Still green with flowerless growth of seedling days,
To build again my city; that no drop
Fallen of these innocent veins on the cold ground
But shall help knit the joints of her firm walls
To knead the stones together, and make sure
The band about her maiden girdlestead
Once fastened, and of all men's violent hands
Inviolable for ever; these to me
Were no such gifts as crave no thanksgiving,
If with one blow dividing the sheer life
I might make end, and one pang wind up all
And seal mine eyes from sorrow; for such end
The Gods give none they love not; but my heart,
That leaps up lightened of all sloth or fear
To take the sword's point, yet with one thought's load
Flags, and falls back, broken of wing, that halts
Maimed in mid flight for thy sake and borne down,
Mother, that in the places where I played
An arm's length from thy bosom and no more
Shalt find me never, nor thine eye wax glad
To mix with mine its eyesight and for love

Laugh without word, filled with sweet light, and speak
Divine dumb things of the inward spirit and heart,
Moved silently; nor hand or lip again
Touch hand or lip of either, but for mine
Shall thine meet only shadows of swift night,
Dreams and dead thoughts of dead things; and the bed
Thou strewedst, a sterile place for all time, strewn
For my sleep only, with its void sad sheets
Shall vex thee, and the unfruitful coverlid
For empty days reproach me dead, that leave
No profit of my body, but am gone
As one not worth being born to bear no seed,
A sapless stock and branchless; yet thy womb
Shall want not honour of me, that brought forth
For all this people freedom, and for earth
From the unborn city born out of my blood
To light the face of all men evermore
Glory; but lay thou this to thy great heart
Whereunder in the dark of birth conceived
Mine unlit life lay girdled with the zone
That bound thy bridal bosom; set this thought
Against all edge of evil as a sword
To beat back sorrow, that for all the world
Thou brought'st me forth a saviour, who shall save
Athens; for none but I from none but thee
Shall take this death for garland; and the men
Mine unknown children of unsounded years,
My sons unrisen shall rise up at thine hand,
Sown of thy seed to bring forth seed to thee,
And call thee most of all most fruitful found
Blessed; but me too for my barren womb
More than my sisters for their children born
Shall these give honour, yea in scorn's own place
Shall men set love and bring for mockery praise
And thanks for curses; for the dry wild vine
Scoffed at and cursed of all men that was I
Shall shed them wine to make the world's heart warm,
That all eyes seeing may lighten, and all ears
Hear and be kindled; such a draught to drink
Shall be the blood that bids this dust bring forth,
The chaliced life here spilt on this mine earth,
Mine, my great father's mother; whom I pray
Take me now gently, tenderly take home,
And softly lay in his my cold chaste hand
Who is called of men by my name, being of Gods
Charged only and chosen to bring men under earth,
And now must lead and stay me with his staff
A silent soul led of a silent God,

Toward sightless things led sightless; and on earth
I see now but the shadow of mine end,
And this last light of all for me in heaven.

PRAXITHEA
Farewell I bid thee; so bid thou not me,
Lest the Gods hear and mock us; yet on these
I lay the weight not of this grief, nor cast
Ill words for ill deeds back; for if one say
They have done men wrong, what hurt have they to hear,
Or he what help to have said it? surely, child,
If one among men born might say it and live
Blameless, none more than I may, who being vexed
Hold yet my peace; for now through tears enough
Mine eyes have seen the sun that from this day
Thine shall see never more; and in the night
Enough has blown of evil, and mine ears
With wail enough the winds have filled, and brought
Too much of cloud from over the sharp sea
To mar for me the morning; such a blast
Rent from these wide void arms and helpless breast
Long since one graft of me disbranched, and bore
Beyond the wild ways of the unwandered world
And loud wastes of the thunder-throated sea,
Springs of the night and openings of the heaven,
The old garden of the Sun; whence never more
From west or east shall winds bring back that blow
From folds of opening heaven or founts of night
The flower of mine once ravished, born my child
To bear strange children; nor on wings of theirs
Shall comfort come back to me, nor their sire
Breathe help upon my peril, nor his strength
Raise up my weakness; but of Gods and men
I drift unsteered on ruin, and the wave
Darkens my head with imminent height, and hangs
Dumb, filled too full with thunder that shall leave
These ears death-deafened when the tide finds tongue
And all its wrath bears on them; thee, O child,
I help not, nor am holpen; fain, ah fain,
More than was ever mother born of man,
Were I to help thee; fain beyond all prayer,
Beyond all thought fain to redeem thee, torn
More timeless from me sorrowing than the dream
That was thy sister; so shalt thou be too,
Thou but a vision, shadow-shaped of sleep,
By grief made out of nothing; now but once
I touch, but once more hold thee, one more kiss
This last time and none other ever more

Leave on thy lips and leave them. Go; thou wast
My heart, my heart's blood, life-blood of my life,
My child, my nursling; now this breast once thine
Shall rear again no children; never now
Shall any mortal blossom born like thee
Lie there, nor ever with small silent mouth
Draw the sweet springs dry for an hour that feed
The blind blithe life that knows not; never head
Rest here to make these cold veins warm, nor eye
Laugh itself open with the lips that reach
Lovingly toward a fount more loving; these
Death makes as all good lesser things now dead,
And all the latter hopes that flowered from these
And fall as these fell fruitless; no joy more
Shall man take of thy maidenhood, no tongue
Praise it; no good shall eyes get more of thee
That lightened for thy love's sake. Now, take note,
Give ear, O all ye people, that my word
May pierce your hearts through, and the stroke that cleaves
Be fruitful to them; so shall all that hear
Grow great at heart with child of thought most high
And bring forth seed in season; this my child,
This flower of this my body, this sweet life,
This fair live youth I give you, to be slain,
Spent, shed, poured out, and perish; take my gift
And give it death and the under Gods who crave
So much for that they give; for this is more,
Much more is this than all we; for they give
Freedom, and for a blast, an air of breath,
A little soul that is not, they give back
Light for all eyes, cheer for all hearts, and life
That fills the world's width full of fame and praise
And mightier love than children's. This they give,
The grace to make thy country great, and wrest
From time and death power to take hold on her
And strength to scathe for ever; and this gift,
Is this no more than man's love is or mine,
Mine and all mothers'? nay, where that seems more,
Where one loves life of child, wife, father, friend,
Son, husband, mother, more than this, even there
Are all these lives worth nothing, all loves else
With this love slain and buried, and their tomb
A thing for shame to spit on; for what love
Hath a slave left to love with? or the heart
Base-born and bound in bondage fast to fear,
What should it do to love thee? what hath he,
The man that hath no country? Gods nor men
Have such to friend, yoked beast-like to base life,

Vile, fruitless, grovelling at the foot of death,
Landless and kinless thralls of no man's blood,
Unchilded and unmothered, abject limbs
That breed things abject; but who loves on earth
Not friend, wife, husband, father, mother, child,
Nor loves his own life for his own land's sake,
But only this thing most, more this than all,
He loves all well and well of all is loved,
And this love lives for ever. See now, friends,
My countrymen, my brothers, with what heart
I give you this that of your hands again
The Gods require for Athens; as I give
So give ye to them what their hearts would have
Who shall give back things better; yea, and these
I take for me to witness, all these Gods,
Were their great will more grievous than it is,
Not one but three, for this one thin-spun thread
A threefold band of children would I give
For this land's love's sake; for whose love to-day
I bid thee, child, fare deathward and farewell.

CHORUS
O wofullest of women, yet of all
Happiest, thy word be hallowed; in all time
Thy name shall blossom, and from strange new tongues
High things be spoken of thee; for such grace
The Gods have dealt to no man, that on none
Have laid so heavy sorrow. From this day
Live thou assured of godhead in thy blood,
And in thy fate no lowlier than a God
In all good things and evil; such a name
Shall be thy child this city's, and thine own
Next hers that called it Athens. Go now forth
Blest, and grace with thee to the doors of death.

CHTHONIA
O city, O glory of Athens, O crown of my father's land, farewell.

CHORUS
For welfare is given her of thee.

CHTHONIA
O Goddess, be good to thy people, that in them dominion and freedom may dwell.

CHORUS
Turn from us the strengths of the sea.

CHTHONIA

Let glory's and theirs be one name in the mouths of all nations made glad with the sun.

CHORUS
For the cloud is blown back with thy breath.

CHTHONIA
With the long last love of mine eyes I salute thee,
O land where my days now are done.

CHORUS
But her life shall be born of thy death.

CHTHONIA
I put on me the darkness thy shadow, my mother, and symbol, O
Earth, of my name.

CHORUS
For thine was her witness from birth.

CHTHONIA
In thy likeness I come to thee darkling, a daughter whose dawn and her even are the same.

CHORUS
Be thine heart to her gracious, O Earth.

CHTHONIA
To thine own kind be kindly, for thy son's name's sake.

CHORUS
That sons unborn may praise thee and thy first-born son.

CHTHONIA
Give me thy sleep, who give thee all my life awake.

CHORUS
Too swift a sleep, ere half the web of day be spun.

CHTHONIA
Death brings the shears or ever life wind up the weft.

CHORUS
Their edge is ground and sharpened; who shall stay his hand?

CHTHONIA
The woof is thin, a small short life, with no thread left.

CHORUS
Yet hath it strength, stretched out, to shelter all the land.

CHTHONIA

Too frail a tent for covering, and a screen too strait.

CHORUS

Yet broad enough for buckler shall thy sweet life be.

CHTHONIA

A little bolt to bar off battle from the gate.

CHORUS

A wide sea-wall, that shatters the besieging sea.

CHTHONIA

I lift up mine eyes from the skirts of the shadow,   **[Strophe.**
From the border of death to the limits of light;
O streams and rivers of mountain and meadow
That hallow the last of my sight,
O father that wast of my mother
Cephisus, O thou too his brother
From the bloom of whose banks as a prey
Winds harried my sister away,
O crown on the world's head lying
Too high for its waters to drown,
Take yet this one word of me dying,
O city, O crown.
Though land-wind and sea-wind with mouths that blow slaughter   **[Antistrophe.**
Should gird them to battle against thee again,
New-born of the blood of a maiden thy daughter,
The rage of their breath shall be vain.
For their strength shall be quenched and made idle,
And the foam of their mouths find a bridle,
And the height of their heads bow down
At the foot of the towers of the town.
Be blest and beloved as I love thee
Of all that shall draw from thee breath;
Be thy life as the sun's is above thee;
I go to my death.

CHORUS

Many loves of many a mood and many a kind   **[Strophe 1.**
Fill the life of man, and mould the secret mind;
Many days bring many dooms, to loose and bind;
Sweet is each in season, good the gift it brings,
Sweet as change of night and day with altering wings,
Night that lulls world-weary day, day that comforts night,

Night that fills our eyes with sleep, day that fills with light.
None of all is lovelier, loftier love is none,   [Antistrophe 1.
Less is bride's for bridegroom, mother's less for son,
Child, than this that crowns and binds up all in one;
Love of thy sweet light, thy fostering breast and hand,
Mother Earth, and city chosen, and natural land;
Hills that bring the strong streams forth, heights of heavenlier air,
Fields aflower with winds and suns, woods with shadowing hair.
But none of the nations of men shall they liken to thee,   [Strophe 2.
Whose children true-born and the fruit of thy body are we.
The rest are thy sons but in figure, in word are thy seed;
We only the flower of thy travail, thy children indeed.
Of thy soil hast thou fashioned our limbs, of thy waters their blood,
And the life of thy springs everlasting is fount of our flood.
No wind oversea blew us hither adrift on thy shore,
None sowed us by land in thy womb that conceived us and bore.
But the stroke of the shaft of the sunlight that brought us to birth
Pierced only and quickened thy furrows to bear us, O Earth.
With the beams of his love wast thou cloven as with iron or fire,
And the life in thee yearned for his life, and grew great with desire.
And the hunger and thirst to be wounded and healed with his dart
Made fruitful the love in thy veins and the depth of thine heart.
And the showers out of heaven overflowing and liquid with love
Fulfilled thee with child of his godhead as rain from above.
Such desire had ye twain of each other, till molten in one   [Antistrophe 2.
Ye might bear and beget of your bodies the fruits of the sun.
And the trees in their season brought forth and were kindled anew
By the warmth of the moisture of marriage, the child-bearing dew.
And the firstlings were fair of the wedlock of heaven and of earth;
All countries were bounteous with blossom and burgeon of birth,
Green pastures of grass for all cattle, and life-giving corn;
But here of thy bosom, here only, the man-child was born.
All races but one are as aliens engrafted or sown,
Strange children and changelings; but we, O our mother, thine own.
Thy nurslings are others, and seedlings they know not of whom;
For these hast thou fostered, but us thou hast borne in thy womb.
Who is he of us all, O beloved, that owe thee for birth,
Who would give not his blood for his birth's sake, O mother, O Earth?
What landsman is he that was fostered and reared of thine hand
Who may vaunt him as we may in death though he die for the land?

Well doth she therefore who gives thee in guerdon
The bloom of the life of thy giving;   [Epode.
And thy body was bowed by no fruitless burden,
That bore such fruit of thee living.
For her face was not darkened for fear,
For her eyelids conceived not a tear,
Nor a cry from her lips craved pity;

But her mouth was a fountain of song,
And her heart as a citadel strong
That guards the heart of the city.

MESSENGER
High things of strong-souled men that loved their land
On brass and stone are written, and their deeds
On high days chanted; but none graven or sung
That ever set men's eyes or spirits on fire,
Athenians, has the sun's height seen, or earth
Heard in her depth reverberate as from heaven,
More worth men's praise and good report of Gods
Than here I bring for record in your ears.
For now being come to the altar, where as priest
Death ministering should meet her, and his hand
Seal her sweet eyes asleep, the maiden stood,
With light in all her face as of a bride
Smiling, or shine of festal flame by night
Far flung from towers of triumph; and her lips
Trembled with pride in pleasure, that no fear
Blanched them nor death before his time drank dry
The blood whose bloom fulfilled them; for her cheeks
Lightened, and brighter than a bridal veil
Her hair enrobed her bosom and enrolled
From face to feet the body's whole soft length
As with a cloud sun-saturate; then she spake
With maiden tongue words manlike, but her eyes
Lit mildly like a maiden's: Countrymen,
With more goodwill and height of happier heart
I give me to you than my mother bare,
And go more gladly this great way to death
Than young men bound to battle. Then with face
Turned to the shadowiest part of all the shrine
And eyes fast set upon the further shade,
Take me, dear Gods; and as some form had shone
From the deep hollow shadow, some God's tongue
Answered, I bless you that your guardian grace
Gives me to guard this country, takes my blood,
Your child's by name, to heal it. Then the priest
Set to the flower-sweet snow of her soft throat
The sheer knife's edge that severed it, and loosed
From the fair bondage of so spotless flesh
So strong a spirit; and all that girt them round
Gazing, with souls that hung on that sad stroke,
Groaned, and kept silence after while a man
Might count how far the fresh blood crept, and bathed
How deep the dark robe and the bright shrine's base
Red-rounded with a running ring that grew

More large and duskier as the wells that fed
Were drained of that pure effluence: but the queen
Groaned not nor spake nor wept, but as a dream
Floats out of eyes awakening so past forth
Ghost-like, a shadow of sorrow, from all sight
To the inner court and chamber where she sits
Dumb, till word reach her of this whole day's end.

CHORUS
More hapless born by far   [Strophe.
Beneath some wintrier star,
One sits in stone among high Lydian snows,
The tomb of her own woes:
Yet happiest was once of the daughters of Gods, and divine by
her sire and her lord,
Ere her tongue was a shaft for the hearts of her sons, for the
heart of her husband a sword.
For she, too great of mind,   [Antistrophe.
Grown through her good things blind.
With godless lips and fire of her own breath
Spake all her house to death;
But thou, no mother unmothered, nor kindled in spirit with pride of thy seed,
Thou hast hallowed thy child for a blameless blood-offering, and ransomed thy race by thy deed.

MESSENGER
As flower is graffed on flower, so grief on grief
Engraffed brings forth new blossoms of strange tears,
Fresh buds and green fruits of an alien pain;
For now flies rumour on a dark wide wing,
Murmuring of woes more than ye knew, most like
Hers whom ye hailed most wretched; for the twain
Last left of all this house that wore last night
A threefold crown of maidens, and to-day
Should let but one fall dead out of the wreath,
If mad with grief we know not and sore love
For this their sister, or with shame soul-stung
To outlive her dead or doubt lest their lives too
The Gods require to seal their country safe
And bring the oracular doom to perfect end,
Have slain themselves, and fallen at the altar-foot
Lie by their own hands done to death; and fear
Shakes all the city as winds a wintering tree,
And as dead leaves are men's hearts blown about
And shrunken with ill thoughts, and flowerless hopes
Parched up with presage, lest the piteous blood
Shed of these maidens guiltless fall and fix
On this land's forehead like a curse that cleaves
To the unclean soul's inexpiate hunted head

Whom his own crime tracks hotlier than a hound
To life's veiled end unsleeping; and this hour
Now blackens toward the battle that must close
All gates of hope and fear on all their hearts
Who tremble toward its issue, knowing not yet
If blood may buy them surety, cleanse or soil
The helpless hands men raise and reach no stay.

CHORUS
Ill thoughts breed fear, and fear ill words; but these
The Gods turn from us that have kept their law.
Let us lift up the strength of our hearts in song,   [Strophe 1.
And our souls to the height of the darkling day.
If the wind in our eyes blow blood for spray,
Be the spirit that breathes in us life more strong,
Though the prow reel round and the helm point wrong,
And sharp reefs whiten the shoreward way.
For the steersman time sits hidden astern,   [Antistrophe 1.
With dark hand plying the rudder of doom,
And the surf-smoke under it flies like fume
As the blast shears off and the oar-blades churn
The foam of our lives that to death return,
Blown back as they break to the gulfing gloom.
What cloud upon heaven is arisen, what shadow, what sound,   [Strophe 2.
From the world beyond earth, from the night underground,
That scatters from wings unbeholden the weight of its darkness around?
For the sense of my spirit is broken, and blinded its eye,   [Antistrophe 2.
As the soul of a sick man ready to die,
With fear of the hour that is on me, with dread if an end be not nigh.
O Earth, O Gods of the land, have ye heart now to see and to hear   [Strophe. 3.
What slays with terror mine eyesight and seals mine ear?
O fountains of streams everlasting, are all ye not shrunk up and withered for fear?
Lo, night is arisen on the noon, and her hounds are in quest by day,   [Antistrophe 3.
And the world is fulfilled of the noise of them crying for their prey,
And the sun's self stricken in heaven, and cast out of his course as a blind man astray.
From east to west of the south sea-line   [Strophe 4.
Glitters the lightning of spears that shine;
As a storm-cloud swoln that comes up from the skirts of the sea
By the wind for helmsman to shoreward ferried,
So black behind them the live storm serried
Shakes earth with the tramp of its foot, and the terror to be.
Shall the sea give death whom the land gave birth?   [Antistrophe 4.
O Earth, fair mother, O sweet live Earth,
Hide us again in thy womb from the waves of it, help us or hide.
As a sword is the heart of the God thy brother,
But thine as the heart of a new-made mother,
To deliver thy sons from his ravin, and rage of his tide.
O strong north wind, the pilot of cloud and rain,   [Strophe 5.

For the gift we gave thee what gift hast thou given us again?
O God dark-winged, deep-throated, a terror to forth-faring ships by night,
What bride-song is this that is blown on the blast of thy breath?
A gift but of grief to thy kinsmen, a song but of death,
For the bride's folk weeping, and woe for her father, who finds thee against him in fight.
Turn back from us, turn thy battle, take heed of our cry;   **[Antistrophe 5.**
Let thy dread breath sound, and the waters of war be dry;
Let thy strong wrath shatter the strength of our foemen, the sword of their strength and the shield;
As vapours in heaven, or as waves or the wrecks of ships,
So break thou the ranks of their spears with the breath of thy lips,
Till their corpses have covered and clothed as with raiment the face of the sword-ploughed field.
O son of the rose-red morning, O God twin-born with the day,   **[Strophe 6.**
O wind with the young sun waking, and winged for the same wide way,
Give up not the house of thy kin to the host thou hast marshalled from northward for prey.
From the cold of thy cradle in Thrace, from the mists of the fountains of night, **[Antistrophe 6.**
From the bride-bed of dawn whence day leaps laughing, on fire for his flight,
Come down with their doom in thine hand on the ships thou hast brought up against us to fight.
For now not in word but in deed is the harvest of spears begun,   **[Strophe 7.**
And its clamour outbellows the thunder, its lightning outlightens the sun
From the springs of the morning it thunders and lightens across and afar
To the wave where the moonset ends and the fall of the last low star.
With a trampling of drenched red hoofs and an earthquake of men that meet,
Strong war sets hand to the scythe, and the furrows take fire from his feet.
Earth groans from her great rent heart, and the hollows of rocks are afraid,
And the mountains are moved, and the valleys as waves in a storm-wind swayed.
From the roots of the hills to the plain's dim verge and the dark loud shore,
Air shudders with shrill spears crossing, and hurtling of wheels that roar.
As the grinding of teeth in the jaws of a lion that foam as they gnash
Is the shriek of the axles that loosen, the shock of the poles that crash.
The dense manes darken and glitter, the mouths of the mad steeds champ,
Their heads flash blind through the battle, and death's foot rings in their tramp.
For a fourfold host upon earth and in heaven is arrayed for the fight,
Clouds ruining in thunder and armies encountering as clouds in the night.
Mine ears are amazed with the terror of trumpets, with darkness mine eyes,
At the sound of the sea's host charging that deafens the roar of the sky's.
White frontlet is dashed upon frontlet, and horse against horse reels hurled,
And the gorge of the gulfs of the battle is wide for the spoil of the world.
And the meadows are cumbered with shipwreck of chariots that founder on land, **[Antistrophe 7.**
And the horsemen are broken with breach as of breakers, and scattered as sand.
Through the roar and recoil of the charges that mingle their cries and confound,
Like fire are the notes of the trumpets that flash through the darkness of sound.
As the swing of the sea churned yellow that sways with the wind as it swells
Is the lift and relapse of the wave of the chargers that clash with their bells;
And the clang of the sharp shrill brass through the burst of the wave as it shocks
Rings clean as the clear wind's cry through the roar of the surge on the rocks:
And the heads of the steeds in their headgear of war, and their corsleted breasts,
Gleam broad as the brows of the billows that brighten the storm with their crests,
Gleam dread as their bosoms that heave to the shipwrecking wind as they rise,

Filled full of the terror and thunder of water, that slays as it dies.
So dire is the glare of their foreheads, so fearful the fire of their breath,
And the light of their eyeballs enkindled so bright with the lightnings of death;
And the foam of their mouths as the sea's when the jaws of its gulf are as graves,
And the ridge of their necks as the wind-shaken mane on the ridges of waves:
And their fetlocks afire as they rear drip thick with a dewfall of blood
As the lips of the rearing breaker with froth of the manslaying flood.
And the whole plain reels and resounds as the fields of the sea by night
When the stroke of the wind falls darkling, and death is the seafarer's light.

But thou, fair beauty of heaven, dear face of the day nigh dead,   [Epode.
What horror hath hidden thy glory, what hand hath muffled thine head?
O sun, with what song shall we call thee, or ward off thy wrath by what name,
With what prayer shall we seek to thee, soothe with what incense, assuage with what gift,
If thy light be such only as lightens to deathward the seaman adrift
With the fire of his house for a beacon, that foemen have wasted with flame?
Arise now, lift up thy light; give ear to us, put forth thine hand,
Reach toward us thy torch of deliverance, a lamp for the night of the land.
Thine eye is the light of the living, no lamp for the dead;
O, lift up the light of thine eye on the dark of our dread.
Who hath blinded thee? who hath prevailed on thee? who hath ensnared?
Who hath broken thy bow, and the shafts for thy battle prepared?
Have they found out a fetter to bind thee, a chain for thine arm that was bared?
Be the name of thy conqueror set forth, and the might of thy master declared.
O God, fair God of the morning, O glory of day,
What ails thee to cast from thy forehead its garland away?
To pluck from thy temples their chaplet enwreathed of the light,
And bind on the brows of thy godhead a frontlet of night?
Thou hast loosened the necks of thine horses, and goaded their flanks with affright,
To the race of a course that we know not on ways that are hid from our sight.
As a wind through the darkness the wheels of their chariot are whirled,
And the light of its passage is night on the face of the world.
And there falls from the wings of thy glory no help from on high,
But a shadow that smites us with fear and desire of thine eye.
For our hearts are as reeds that a wind on the water bows down and goes by,
To behold not thy comfort in heaven that hath left us untimely to die.
But what light is it now leaps forth on the land
Enkindling the waters and ways of the air
From thy forehead made bare,
From the gleam of thy bow-bearing hand?
Hast thou set not thy right hand again to the string,
With the back-bowed horns bent sharp for a spring
And the barbed shaft drawn,
Till the shrill steel sing and the tense nerve ring
That pierces the heart of the dark with dawn,
O huntsman, O king,
When the flame of thy face hath twilight in chase
As a hound hath a blood-mottled fawn?

He has glanced into golden the grey sea-strands,
And the clouds are shot through with the fires of his hands,
And the height of the hollow of heaven that he fills
As the heart of a strong man is quickened and thrills;
High over the folds of the low-lying lands,
On the shadowless hills
As a guard on his watchtower he stands.
All earth and all ocean, all depth and all height,
At the flash of an eyebeam are filled with his might:
The sea roars backward, the storm drops dumb,
And silence as dew on the fire of the fight
Falls kind in our ears as his face in our sight
With presage of peace to come.
Fresh hope in my heart from the ashes of dread
Leaps clear as a flame from the pyres of the dead,
That joy out of woe
May arise as the spring out of tempest and snow,
With the flower-feasted month in her hands rose-red
Borne soft as a babe from the bearing-bed.
Yet it knows not indeed if a God be friend,
If rescue may be from the rage of the sea,
Or the wrath of its lord have end.
For the season is full now of death or of birth,
To bring forth life, or an end of all;
And we know not if anything stand or fall
That is girdled about with the round sea's girth
As a town with its wall;
But thou that art highest of the Gods most high,
That art lord if we live, that art lord though we die,
Have heed of the tongues of our terror that cry
For a grace to the children of Earth.

ATHENIAN HERALD
Sons of Athens, heavy-laden with the holy weight of years,
Be your hearts as young men's lightened of their loathlier load of fears;
For the wave is sunk whose thunder shoreward shook the shuddering lands,
And unbreached of warring waters Athens like a sea-rock stands.

CHORUS
Well thy word has cheered us, well thy face and glittering eyes, that spake
Ere thy tongue spake words of comfort: yet no pause, behoves it make
Till the whole good hap find utterance that the Gods have given at length.

ATHENIAN HERALD
All is this, that yet the city stands unforced by stranger strength.

CHORUS
Sweeter sound might no mouth utter in man's ear than this thy word.

ATHENIAN HERALD.
Feed thy soul then full of sweetness till some bitterer note be heard.

CHORUS
None, if this ring sure, can mar the music fallen from heaven as rain.

ATHENIAN HERALD.
If no fire of sun or star untimely sear the tender grain.

CHORUS
Fresh the dewfall of thy tidings on our hopes reflowering lies.

ATHENIAN HERALD
Till a joyless shower and fruitless blight them, raining from thine eyes.

CHORUS
Bitter springs have barren issues; these bedew grief's arid sands.

ATHENIAN HERALD
Such thank-offerings ask such altars as expect thy suppliant hands.

CHORUS
Tears for triumph, wail for welfare, what strange godhead's shrine requires?

ATHENIAN HERALD.
Death's or victory's be it, a funeral torch feeds all its festal fires.

CHORUS
Like a star should burn the beacon flaming from our city's head.

ATHENIAN HERALD
Like a balefire should the flame go up that says the king is dead.

CHORUS
Out of heaven, a wild-haired meteor, shoots this new sign, scattering fear.

ATHENIAN HERALD
Yea, the word has wings of fire that hovered, loth to burn thine ear.

CHORUS
From thy lips it leapt forth loosened on a shrill and shadowy wing.

ATHENIAN HERALD
Long they faltered, fain to hide it deep as death that hides the king.

CHORUS
Dead with him blind hope lies blasted by the lightning of one sword.

ATHENIAN HERALD

On thy tongue truth wars with error; no man's edge hath touched thy lord.

CHORUS

False was thine then, jangling menace like a war-steed's brow-bound bell?

ATHENIAN HERALD

False it rang not joy nor sorrow; but by no man's hand he fell.

CHORUS

Vainly then good news and evil through so faint a trumpet spake.

ATHENIAN HERALD

All too long thy soul yet labours, as who sleeping fain would wake,
Waking, fain would fall on sleep again; the woe thou knowest not yet,
When thou knowest, shall make thy memory thirst and hunger to forget.

CHORUS

Long my heart has hearkened, hanging on thy clamorous ominous cry,
Fain yet fearful of the knowledge whence it looks to live or die;
Now to take the perfect presage of thy dark and sidelong flight
Comes a surer soothsayer sorrowing, sable-stoled as birds of night.

PRAXITHEA

Man, what thy mother bare thee born to say
Speak; for no word yet wavering on thy lip
Can wound me worse than thought forestalls or fear.

ATHENIAN HERALD

I have no will to weave too fine or far,
O queen, the weft of sweet with bitter speech,
Bright words with darkling; but the brief truth shown
Shall plead my pardon for a lingering tongue,
Loth yet to strike hope through the heart and slay.
The sun's light still was lordly housed in heaven
When the twain fronts of war encountering smote
First fire out of the battle; but not long
Had the fresh wave of windy fight begun
Heaving, and all the surge of swords to sway,
When timeless night laid hold of heaven, and took
With its great gorge the noon as in a gulf,
Strangled; and thicker than the shrill-winged shafts
Flew the fleet lightnings, held in chase through heaven
By headlong heat of thunders on their trail
Loosed as on quest of quarry; that our host
Smit with sick presage of some wrathful God
Quailed, but the foe as from one iron throat

With one great sheer sole thousand-throated cry
Shook earth, heart-staggered from their shout, and clove
The eyeless hollow of heaven; and breached therewith
As with an onset of strength-shattering sound
The rent vault of the roaring noon of night
From her throned seat of usurpation rang
Reverberate answer; such response there pealed
As though the tide's charge of a storming sea
Had burst the sky's wall, and made broad a breach
In the ambient girth and bastion flanked with stars
Guarding the fortress of the Gods, and all
Crashed now together on ruin; and through that cry
And higher above it ceasing one man's note
Tore its way like a trumpet: Charge, make end,
Charge, halt not, strike, rend up their strength by the roots,
Strike, break them, make your birthright's promise sure,
Show your hearts hardier than the fenced land breeds
And souls breathed in you from no spirit of earth,
Sons of the sea's waves; and all ears that heard
Rang with that fiery cry, that the fine air
Thereat was fired, and kindling filled the plain
Full of that fierce and trumpet-quenching breath
That spake the clarions silent; no glad song
For folk to hear that wist how dire a God
Begat this peril to them, what strong race
Fathered the sea-born tongue that sang them death,
Threatening; so raged through the red foam of fight
Poseidon's son Eumolpus; and the war
Quailed round him coming, and our side bore back,
As a stream thwarted by the wind and sea
That meet it midway mouth to mouth, and beat
The flood back of its issue; but the king
Shouted against them, crying, O Father-God,
Source of the God my father, from thine hand
Send me what end seems good now in thy sight,
But death from mine to this man; and the word
Quick on his lips yet like a blast of fire
Blew them together; and round its lords that met
Paused all the reeling battle; two main waves
Meeting, one hurled sheer from the sea-wall back
That shocks it sideways, one right in from sea
Charging, that full in face takes at one blow
That whole recoil and ruin, with less fear
Startle men's eyes late shipwrecked; for a breath
Crest fronting crest hung, wave to wave rose poised,
Then clashed, breaker to breaker; cloud with cloud
In heaven, chariot with chariot closed on earth,
One fourfold flash and thunder; yet a breath,

And with the king's spear through his red heart's root
Driven, like a rock split from its hill-side, fell
Hurled under his own horsehoofs dead on earth
The sea-beast that made war on earth from sea,
Dumb, with no shrill note left of storming song,
Eumolpus; and his whole host with one stroke
Spear-stricken through its dense deep iron heart
Fell hurtling from us, and in fierce recoil
Drew seaward as with one wide wail of waves,
Resorbed with reluctation; such a groan
Rose from the fluctuant refluence of its ranks,
Sucked sullen back and strengthless; but scarce yet
The steeds had sprung and wheels had bruised their lord
Fallen, when from highest height of the sundering heaven
The Father for his brother's son's sake slain
Sent a sheer shaft of lightning writhen and smote
Right on his son's son's forehead, that unhelmed
Shone like the star that shines down storm, and gave
Light to men's eyes that saw thy lord their king
Stand and take breath from battle; then too soon
Saw sink down as a sunset in sea-mist
The high bright head that here in van of the earth
Rose like a headland, and through storm and night
Took all the sea's wrath on it; and now dead
They bring thee back by war-forsaken ways
The strength called once thy husband, the great guard
That was of all men, stay of all men's lives,
They bear him slain of no man but a God,
Godlike; and toward him dead the city's gates
Fling their arms open mother-like, through him
Saved; and the whole clear land is purged of war.
What wilt thou say now of this weal and woe?

PRAXITHEA
I praise the Gods for Athens. O sweet Earth,
Mother, what joy thy soul has of thy son,
Thy life of my dead lord, mine own soul knows
That knows thee godlike; and what grief should mine,
What sorrow should my heart have, who behold
Thee made so heavenlike happy? This alone
I only of all these blessed, all thy kind,
Crave this for blessing to me, that in theirs
Have but a part thus bitter; give me too
Death, and the sight of eyes that meet not mine.
And thee too from no godless heart or tongue
Reproachful, thee too by thy living name,
Father divine, merciful God, I call,
Spring of my life-springs, fountain of my stream,

Pure and poured forth to one great end with thine,
Sweet head sublime of triumph and these tears,
Cephisus, if thou seest as gladly shed
Thy blood in mine as thine own waves are given
To do this great land good, to give for love
The same lips drink and comfort the same hearts,
Do thou then, O my father, white-souled God,
To thy most pure earth-hallowing heart eterne
Take what thou gavest to be given for these,
Take thy child to thee; for her time is full,
For all she hath borne she hath given, seen all she had
Flow from her, from her eyes and breasts and hands
Flow forth to feed this people; but be thou,
Dear God and gracious to all souls alive,
Good to thine own seed also; let me sleep,
Father; my sleepless darkling day is done,
My day of life like night, but slumberless:
For all my fresh fair springs, and his that ran
In one stream's bed with mine, are all run out
Into the deep of death. The Gods have saved
Athens; my blood has bought her at their hand,
And ye sit safe; be glorious and be glad
As now for all time always, countrymen,
And love my dead for ever; but me, me,
What shall man give for these so good as death?

CHORUS

From the cup of my heart I pour through my lips along   **[Strophe 1.**
The mingled wine of a joyful and sorrowful song;
Wine sweeter than honey and bitterer than blood that is poured
From the chalice of gold, from the point of the two-edged sword.
For the city redeemed should joy flow forth as a flood,
And a dirge make moan for the city polluted with blood.
Great praise should the Gods have surely, my country, of thee,   **[Antistrophe 1.**
Were thy brow but as white as of old for thy sons to see,
Were thy hands as bloodless, as blameless thy cheek divine;
But a stain on it stands of the life-blood offered for thine.
What thanks shall we give that are mixed not and marred with dread
For the price that has ransomed thine own with thine own child's head?
For a taint there cleaves to the people redeemed with blood,   **[Strophe 2.**
And a plague to the blood-red hand.
The rain shall not cleanse it, the dew nor the sacred flood
That blesses the glad live land.
In the darkness of earth beneath, in the world without sun,   **[Antistrophe 2.**
The shadows of past things reign;
And a cry goes up from the ghost of an ill deed done,
And a curse for a virgin slain.

ATHENA

Hear, men that mourn, and woman without mate,
Hearken; ye sick of soul with fear, and thou
Dumb-stricken for thy children; hear ye too,
Earth, and the glory of heaven, and winds of the air,
And the most holy heart of the deep sea,
Late wroth, now full of quiet; hear thou, sun,
Rolled round with the upper fire of rolling heaven
And all the stars returning; hills and streams,
Springs and fresh fountains, day that seest these deeds.
Night that shalt hide not; and thou child of mine,
Child of a maiden, by a maid redeemed,
Blood-guiltless, though bought back with innocent blood,
City mine own; I Pallas bring thee word,
I virgin daughter of the most high God
Give all you charge and lay command on all
The word I bring be wasted not; for this
The Gods have stablished and his soul hath sworn,
That time nor earth nor changing sons of man
Nor waves of generations, nor the winds
Of ages risen and fallen that steer their tides
Through light and dark of birth and lovelier death
From storm toward haven inviolable, shall see
So great a light alive beneath the sun
As the awless eye of Athens; all fame else
Shall be to her fame as a shadow in sleep
To this wide noon at waking; men most praised
In lands most happy for their children found
Shall hold as highest of honours given of God
To be but likened to the least of thine,
Thy least of all, my city; thine shall be
The crown of all songs sung, of all deeds done
Thine the full flower for all time; in thine hand
Shall time be like a sceptre, and thine head
Wear worship for a garland; nor one leaf
Shall change or winter cast out of thy crown
Till all flowers wither in the world; thine eyes
Shall first in man's flash lightning liberty,
Thy tongue shall first say freedom; thy first hand
Shall loose the thunder terror as a hound
To hunt from sunset to the springs of the sun
Kings that rose up out of the populous east
To make their quarry of thee, and shall strew
With multitudinous limbs of myriad herds
The foodless pastures of the sea, and make
With wrecks immeasurable and unsummed defeat
One ruin of all their many-folded flocks
Ill shepherded from Asia; by thy side

Shall fight thy son the north wind, and the sea
That was thine enemy shall be sworn thy friend
And hand be struck in hand of his and thine
To hold faith fast for aye; with thee, though each
Make war on other, wind and sea shall keep
Peace, and take truce as brethren for thy sake
Leagued with one spirit and single-hearted strength
To break thy foes in pieces, who shall meet
The wind's whole soul and might of the main sea
Full in their face of battle, and become
A laughter to thee; like a shower of leaves
Shall their long galleys rank by staggering rank
Be dashed adrift on ruin, and in thy sight
The sea deride them, and that lord of the air
Who took by violent hand thy child to wife
With his loud lips bemock them, by his breath
Swept out of sight of being; so great a grace
Shall this day give thee, that makes one in heart
With mine the deep sea's godhead, and his son
With him that was thine helmsman, king with king,
Dead man with dead; such only names as these
Shalt thou call royal, take none else or less
To hold of men in honour; but with me
Shall these be worshipped as one God, and mix
With mine the might of their mysterious names
In one same shrine served singly, thence to keep
Perpetual guard on Athens; time and change,
Masters and lords of all men, shall be made
To thee that knowest no master and no lord
Servants; the days that lighten heaven and nights
That darken shall be ministers of thine
To attend upon thy glory, the great years
As light-engraven letters of thy name
Writ by the sun's hand on the front of the earth
For world-beholden witness; such a gift
For one fair chaplet of three lives enwreathed
To hang for ever from thy storied shrine,
And this thy steersman fallen with tiller in hand
To stand for ever at thy ship's helm seen,
Shall he that bade their threefold flower be shorn
And laid him low that planted, give thee back
In sign of sweet land reconciled with sea
And heavenlike earth with heaven; such promise-pledge
I daughter without mother born of God
To the most woful mother born of man
Plight for continual comfort. Hail, and live
Beyond all human hap of mortal doom
Happy; for so my sire hath sworn and I.

PRAXITHEA

O queen Athena, from a heart made whole
Take as thou givest us blessing; never tear
Shall stain for shame nor groan untune the song
That as a bird shall spread and fold its wings
Here in thy praise for ever, and fulfil
The whole world's crowning city crowned with thee
As the sun's eye fulfils and crowns with sight
The circling crown of heaven. There is no grief
Great as the joy to be made one in will
With him that is the heart and rule of life
And thee, God born of God; thy name is ours,
And thy large grace more great than our desire.

CHORUS

From the depth of the springs of my spirit a fountain is poured of thanksgiving,
My country, my mother, for thee,
That thy dead for their death shall have life in thy sight and a name everliving
At heart of thy people to be.
In the darkness of change on the waters of time they shall turn from afar
To the beam of this dawn for a beacon, the light of these pyres for a star.
They shall see thee who love and take comfort, who hate thee shall see and take warning,
Our mother that makest us free;
And the sons of thine earth shall have help of the waves that made war on their morning,
And friendship and fame of the sea.

Algernon Charles Swinburne – A Short Biography

Algernon Charles Swinburne was born at 7 Chester Street, Grosvenor Place, in London, on April 5th, 1837. He was the eldest of six children born to Captain Charles Henry Swinburne and Lady Jane Henrietta, daughter of the 3rd Earl of Ashburnham, a wealthy Northumbrian family.

Swinburne spent his early years at East Dene in Bonchurch, on the Isle of Wight. As a child, Swinburne was nervous and frail, but also imbued with a nervous energy and fearlessness almost to the point of recklessness.

He was schooled at Eton College from 1849 to 1853. It was here that he first began to write poetry. He excelled at languages and whilst still at Eton won first prizes in both French and Italian.

From Eton he moved to Oxford where he attended at Balliol College from 1856. Here he met friends to whom he became closely attached, among them Dante Gabriel Rossetti, William Morris and Edward Burne-Jones, who in 1857, were painting their Arthurian murals on the walls of the Oxford Union. At Oxford Swinburne was mentored by Benjamin Jowett, the master of Balliol College, who recognised his poetic talent and, intervening on his behalf, tried to keep him from being expelled when he celebrated the Italian patriot Orsini, and his failed attempt on the life of Napoleon III in 1858. Swinburne had to leave the Universcity for a few months due to this but returned in May, 1860 but never received a degree.

Summers were usually spent at Capheaton Hall in Northumberland, the house of his grandfather, Sir John Swinburne, 6th Baronet, who had a famous library and was himself President of the Literary and Philosophical Society in Newcastle upon Tyne.

Swinburne proudly considered himself a native of Northumberland and this is reflected in poems such as the intensely patriotic 'Northumberland' and 'Grace Darling'. He enjoyed riding across the moors and was, it was said, a daring horseman, as he moved 'through honeyed leagues of the northland border', as he remembered the Scottish border in his Recollections.

In the period from 1857 to 1860, Swinburne was one of a number of Pre-Raphaelite's who visited and became part of Lady Pauline Trevelyan's intellectual circle at Wallington Hall, a few miles west of Morpeth in Northumberland.

After leaving college, he moved to London and began his career in earnest as well as becoming a constant visitor to the Rossetti's house. To Rossetti Swinburne was his 'little Northumbrian friend', an affectionate reference to Swinburne's small stature—a mere five foot four. Whatever Swinburne lacked in height he made up for in poetic talent. However, with the burden of such great talent came the unveiling of a dark side that was to cause him pain and would, at times, threaten his very existence with all manner of self-inflicted pains through drink, drugs and sado-machoism.

In 1860 Swinburne published two verse dramas; The Queen Mother and Rosamond but it would not be until 1865 that Swinburne would achieve literary success with Atalanta in Calydon.

In 1861, Swinburne visited Menton on the French Riviera to recover from the effects of yet another period of excess use of alcohol, staying at the Villa Laurenti. From Menton, Swinburne then travelled on to Italy, where he journeyed widely.

After Elizabeth Rossetti's death from suicide in 1862, he and Rossetti moved to Tudor House at 16 Cheyne Walk in Chelsea. The stories that survive from his year with Rossetti are typical Swinburne. In one, Rossetti once had to tell him to keep down the noise — he and a boyfriend had been sliding naked down the bannisters and disturbing Rossetti's painting. He took a sardonic delight in what the critic and biographer, Cecil Lang, calls "Algernonic exaggeration": When people began to talk scathingly about his homosexuality and other sexual proclivities, he circulated a story that he had engaged in pederasty and bestiality with a monkey — and then eaten it. How many of the stories were true and how many invented is unclear. Oscar Wilde called him "a braggart in matters of vice, who had done everything he could to convince his fellow citizens of his homosexuality and bestiality without being in the slightest degree a homosexual or a bestialiser."

In December 1862, Swinburne accompanied Scott and his guests on a trip to Tynemouth. Scott writes in his memoirs that, as they walked by the sea, Swinburne declaimed the as yet unpublished 'Hymn to Proserpine' and 'Laus Veneris' in his lilting intonation, while the waves 'were running the whole length of the long level sands towards Cullercoats and sounding like far-off acclamations'.

Swinburne possessed a curious combination of frail health and strength. He was small and slightly built, but an excellent swimmer and the first to climb Culver Cliff on the Isle of Wight. He had an extremely excitable disposition: people who met him described him as a "demoniac boy" who would go skipping about the room declaiming poetry at the top of his voice. In this as in many things, moderation was not the standard for him. Excess was. Once or twice he had fits, thought to be epileptic, in public; but he made this condition much worse by drinking past excess to unconsciousness. More than once he was delivered to the door in the small of the night, dead drunk. Throughout the 1860s and '70s he rode an alcoholic cycle of dissolution, collapse, drying out at home in the country, then returning to London where he would begin the cycle all over again.

His mania for masochism, particularly flagellation, most probably started in early childhood at Eton and was encouraged by his later friendships with Richard Monckton Milnes (one of Tennyson's fellow Apostles), who introduced him to the works of the Marquis de Sade, and Richard Burton, the Victorian explorer and adventurer. Swinburne was an alcoholic and algolagniac (a desire for sexual gratification through inflicting pain on oneself or others; sadomasochism). He found life difficult, unfulfilling but still his poetic talents pushed to the fore.

Although Swinburne continued to publish some works in periodicals in 1865 he was granted recognition by both public and critics with Atalanta in Calydon written in the style of a classical Greek tragedy.

There followed "Laus Veneris" and Poems and Ballads (1866), with their sexually charged passages, absolutely decadent for polite Victorian society, which were attacked all the more violently as a result. The poems written in homage of Sappho of Lesbos such as "Anactoria" and "Sapphics" were especially savaged. The volume also contained poems such as "The Leper," "Laus Veneris," and "St Dorothy" which evoke both Swinburne's and a general Victorian fascination with the Middle Ages, and are explicitly mediaeval in style, tone and construction. With its publication came instant notoriety. He was now identified with indecent and decadent themes and the precept of art for art's sake.

Swinburne's meeting in 1867 with his long-time hero Mazzini, the Italian patriot living in England in exile, was the beginning of a poetical journey that now became more serious and more engaged with serious thought, initially leading to the political poems in the volume Songs Before Sunrise.

Also in 1867 he was introduced to Adah Isaacs Menken, the American actress, poet and circus rider, whose main fame seemed to be riding naked on a horse (in fact she wore tight nude coloured clothing) for her performance in the melodrama Mazeppa (itself based on a poem by Lord Byron). Although they had a short affair Adah's quote implies that Swinburne was not ready for a relationship that did not involve some self-sabotage; "I can't make him understand that biting's no use."

In 1879, with Swinburne nearly dead from alcoholism and dissolution, his legal advisor Theodore Watts-Dunton took him in, and was gradually successful in getting him to adapt to a healthier lifestyle. Swinburne lived the rest of his life at Watts-Dunton's house. He saw less and less of his old bohemian friends, who thought him a prisoner at The Pines, but his growing deafness also accounts for some of his decreased sociability. By now Swinburne was 42, and was moving from a young man of rebelliousness to a figure of social respectability. It was said of Watts-Dunton that he saved the man and killed the poet.

It is clear that Swinburne had an addictive personality, and clearly incapable of moderation in his pursuit of any chosen vices. This, of course, would both nourish and perhaps sabotage his poetic career. His poetry follows the somewhat clichéd pattern of early flourish and later decline; indeed some of the fresher pieces in the second and third series of Poems and Ballads (published in 1878 and 1889) were actually written during his days at Oxford. Nevertheless, his last collection, A Channel Passage, has some beautiful poems, including "The Lake of Gaube."

He is best remembered as the supreme technician in metre, with a versatility which exceeds even Tennyson's, but which lacks a corresponding emotional range. His obsessions are not widely enough shared; and if he cannot shock us by the strangeness of his desires nor the shrillness of his anti-theistical exclamations, often what remains is not enough to fully engage with the audience.

Swinburne is considered a poet of the decadent school, although he perhaps professed to more vice than he actually indulged in to advertise his deviance. Common gossip of the time reported that he also had a deep crush on the explorer Sir Richard Francis Burton, despite the fact that Swinburne himself abhorred travel. Fact and fiction are easily absorbed by the other so are difficult to untangle even now.

Many critics consider his mastery of vocabulary, rhyme and metre impressive, although he has also been criticised for his florid style and word choices that only fit the rhyme scheme rather than contributing to the meaning of the piece. A. E. Housman, although a critic, had great praise for his rhyming ability: to Swinburne the sonnet was child's play: the task of providing four rhymes was not hard enough, and he wrote long poems in which each stanza required eight or ten rhymes, and wrote them so that he never seemed to be saying anything for the rhyme's sake.

Throughout his career Swinburne published literary criticism of great worth. His deep knowledge of world literatures contributed to a critical style rich in quotation, allusion, and comparison. He is particularly noted for discerning studies of Elizabethan dramatists and of many English and French poets and novelists. As well he was a noted essayist and wrote two novels.

Swinburne was nominated for the Nobel Prize in Literature every year from 1903 to 1907 and then again in 1909.

H.P. Lovecraft, the master of the dark side and a decent poet himself, considered Swinburne "the only real poet in either England or America after the death of Mr. Edgar Allan Poe."

Swinburne was also responsible for devising a poetic form called the roundel, a variation of the French Rondeau form. In 1883 he published A Century of Roundels with several of the roundels dedicated to Dante's sister, the poet Christina Georgina Rossetti. Swinburne wrote to Edward Burne-Jones in 1883: "I have got a tiny new book of songs or songlets, in one form and all manner of metres ... just coming out, of which Miss Rossetti has accepted the dedication. I hope you and Georgie [his wife Georgiana] will find something to like among a hundred poems of nine lines each, twenty-four of which are about babies or small children".

Opinions of the Roundel poems move between those who find them captivating and brilliant, to others who find them merely clever and contrived. One of them, A Baby's Death, was set to music by the English composer Sir Edward Elgar as the song "Roundel: The little eyes that never knew Light".

After the first Poems and Ballads, Swinburne's later poetry was devoted more to philosophy and politics, including the unification of Italy, particularly in the volume Songs before Sunrise. He did not stop writing love poetry entirely, indeed it was only in 1882 that his great epic-length poem, Tristram of Lyonesse, was published, its contents lyrical rather than shocking. His versification, and especially his rhyming technique, remain of high quality to the end.

Algernon Charles Swinburne died of influenza, at the Pines in London on April 10th, 1909 at the age of 72. He was buried at St. Boniface Church, Bonchurch on the Isle of Wight.

Algernon Charles Swinburne – A Concise Bibliography

Verse Drama
The Queen Mother (1860)
Rosamond (1860)
Chastelard (1865)
Bothwell (1874)
Mary Stuart (1881)
Marino Faliero (1885)
Locrine (1887)
The Sisters (1892)
Rosamund, Queen of the Lombards (1899)

Poetry
Atalanta in Calydon (1865)*
Poems and Ballads (1866)
Songs Before Sunrise (1871)
Songs of Two Nations (1875)
Erechtheus (1876)*
Poems and Ballads, Second Series (1878)
Songs of the Springtides (1880)
Studies in Song (1880)
The Heptalogia, or the Seven against Sense. A Cap with Seven Bells (1880)
Tristram of Lyonesse (1882)
A Dark Month & Other Poems
A Century of Roundels (1883)
A Midsummer Holiday and Other Poems (1884)
Poems and Ballads, Third Series (1889)
Astrophel and Other Poems (1894)
The Tale of Balen (1896)
A Channel Passage and Other Poems (1904)

*Although formally tragedies, Atlanta in Calydon and Erechtheus are traditionally included with his poetry.

Criticism
William Blake: A Critical Essay (1868, new edition 1906)
Under the Microscope (1872)
George Chapman: A Critical Essay (1875)
Essays and Studies (1875)
A Note on Charlotte Brontë (1877)
A Study of Shakespeare (1880)

A Study of Victor Hugo (1886)
A Study of Ben Johnson (1889)
Studies in Prose and Poetry (1894)
The Age of Shakespeare (1908)
Shakespeare (1909)

Major Collections
The Poems of Algernon Charles Swinburne, 6 vols. 1904.
The Tragedies of Algernon Charles Swinburne, 5 vols. 1905.
The Complete Works of Algernon Charles Swinburne, 20 vols. Bonchurch Edition. 1925-7.
The Swinburne Letters, 6 vols. 1959-62.

www.ingramcontent.com/pod-product-compliance
Lightning Source LLC
Chambersburg PA
CBHW070111070426
42448CB00038B/2507